5 Surprising Steps to Land the Job NOW!

KRISTIN SHERRY

Published by Virtus Career Consulting, Charlotte, North Carolina.

ISBN: 9781979618700
ISBN: 1979618704
Library of Congress Control Number: 2017918387
Cover design by Crystal Davies, Davies Designs
Edited by Beth Crosby

This publication is designed to provide accurate and authoritative information regarding the
subject matter covered. It is sold with the understanding that the publisher is not engaged in
rendering legal, accounting, or other professional services. If legal advice or other expert assis-

tance is required, the services of a competent professional person should be sought.

WHAT KRISTIN'S CLIENTS ARE SAYING...

"Kristin sets herself apart as a career coach. She can quickly assess the situation and provide great insight that leads to a positive result. I consider Kristin a great partner who will help you achieve greater success in life. With her partnership, I landed my dream job."

— **Ting Zhao**

"Today's talent acquisition requires many titles and sometimes departments to truly vet a candidate. Interviewing can be a lengthy and daunting process. I was impressed with Kristin's ability to help me navigate each interviewer. She coached me on which facets of my strengths, talents and experiences each set of eyes was looking for. In the end, this strategy won me the job."

— **Mead Poncin**

"I got an in-person interview for a job I really wanted and met with Kristin to go over interviewing strategies. I left our meeting feeling much more confident and prepared. Once I got to the interview, I felt much calmer and more relaxed than I would have without her help. Many of the points she mentioned were brought up in the interview, and I was able to give clear, concise answers to the questions. And, I got the job!"

— **Michele Reader**

"I was downsized after 27 years working for one company in a very industry specific role. Kristin helped me identify my strengths and weaknesses and how I could apply them to the type of role that best suited my personality. Her advice and enthusiasm in my abilities propelled me to apply for and land my dream job. Being confident in one's skills and abilities is not enough, being able to present the complete package to the hiring manager to set oneself apart from other candidates is so vital and I thank Kristin for her help in helping me reach my potential."

– Caroline L.

"My work with Kristin not only helped me realize my true strengths I bring to the workplace, but gave me the confidence to express them during interviews, as well. As a result, I landed a job very shortly after, and could not be happier. Working together was easily one of the best investments I've made in myself."

– Holly Exposito

"Like most people, I used to dread the interview process and would try to schedule interviews for the last day available. Since working with Kristin Sherry, I am empowered and always ready for an interview or elevator conversation. Her methodology helps you tailor your qualifications and strengths to the job at hand, gain the attention of recruiters and influencers, and has placed me in a position where I am doing what I love with the people I want to work with."

– Roxanne Arriaza

"I highly recommend Kristin as an excellent resource in any career change/job search. She was critical in my interview preparation by compiling information about me and determining how best to relay my total story to a future employer. The asset summary she put together reflecting my strengths, talents and personality was instrumental in my gaining a final interview with the company that I desired to work with and ultimately resulted in an offer. Kristin is professional, personable and fun to work with. She has savvy and creativity when it comes to building a total profile picture and 'wowing' a future employer."

– Kelly L.

"Working with Kristin was an enlightening experience. I learned so much about myself and how to present myself to others. I love how she helped me navigate awkward discussions like salary requirements and why I separated from my previous employer. The interview guide is also amazing and helps me feel prepared for each interview. Each session also helped me learn to frame my strengths, values and experiences in a coherent and marketable way. Kristin exceeded my expectations and I have already recommended her to others looking to make a career change."

– Nicole Young

"Kristin worked with me to identify the confluence of my own skills, likes and dislikes, which helped me define specific parameters for my job search. She then went on to provide coaching on how to prepare for interviews and practice my interviewing skills. The YouMap summary Kristin prepared is a tool I continue to update in the event I need to look for a new role in the future.

Kristin is a quintessential Career Coach who was both candid about my opportunities for improvement and still a great cheerleader for my successes.

The bottom line is, I found a better job, the *right* job for me, largely based on finding the right role for my skills and passion that Kristin helped me discern."

— **Christopher Kubala**

"Kristin helped me better understand my strengths and build a summary of my assets. I definitely feel more confident and share the summary with all my clients."

— **Mueed Mohammed**

"After working with Kristin, I had a resurgence of confidence and enthusiasm because I *knew* I had unique value to offer and how to articulate it succinctly. Work with Kristin! It's an investment in yourself and your future."

— **Katy Mooney**

"I'm thankful in the midst of changing jobs to have had the chance to work with someone who was so knowledgeable, encouraging and funny. Being able to integrate what is with what can be was an insightful process that not only led me to a new job, but also an increased awareness of how I tick and how that affects all my interactions. I experienced both peace and excitement through the roller coaster ride. It just wouldn't have been fun without Kristin!"

— **Stephanie Boschee**

"I have been around the interviewing block, but finally took another avenue when I met Kristin. She has changed the landscape of how I interview from providing comprehensive tools I can use when preparing for any type of interview to one-on-one meetings where we discuss solutions for very specific challenges at each company. Her knowledge and advice are excellent, her manner is direct yet friendly, and her attitude is always positive. Because of her coaching, I have had more interviews and more second interviews. I know I am on the right road to a new job!"

– Denise S.

"UNBELIEVABLE! The most valuable information I have ever seen or read concerning the subject of interviewing."

– Sharon Sasser

"Kristin helped me to identify the skills and talents that I already possessed and relate them to skills that were needed in my new career choice. She helped me to construct my evidence-based stories so that they demonstrated my skills and how they would lead to my success in a new position. Kristin helped me to see my value and how I could change the focus of my career from academics to the business world. She made me believe that I could, and I did."

– Mia M-O.

To my husband, Xander — you've helped me grow to become a better version of myself. I love you. You're my favorite!

CONTENTS

FOREWORD

When one of my best friends, Ryan, asked me to help him transition his fifteen-year entrepreneurial career in China to a management job back in the United States, I said, "I think there is someone better."

I referred him to Kristin Sherry.

From the first time I met Kristin through our church career ministry several years ago, I was blown away by her focus and insight into people, and their gifts and passions. I discovered her professional career had grown from a .NET software developer to Learning and Development Manager for the patient support services division of AmerisourceBergen, one of the largest healthcare companies in the world.

Then, she took a leap of faith into her own business, Virtus Career Consulting. This past year, she published a refreshing and relevant book about career success strategies titled *Follow Your Star.*

As the founder of Crossroads Career Network, I believe Kristin is one of the standout volunteer coaches and speakers helping more than 50,000 registered users on the Crossroads Career ministry website, which is dedicated to helping people get the right job, maximize their career, and follow God's calling. In my forty-year career in executive search, human resources, and now ministry, I am continuing to learn more and better ways from Kristin to help people walk in good works.

Kristin's new book, *5 Surprising Steps to Land the Job NOW!,* gets into the weeds of how to actually turn interviews into offers. It is a quick read, even an entertaining book, on the serious challenges of getting the job you want. Filled with proven principles and practical applications, you can learn interview techniques and use the latest tools to help land the job now!

As for my friend Ryan, he is a happy career explorer, having completed discovery of his strengths and is now focused on specific potential employers and how he can help them succeed.

Blessings for the Day,

Brian Ray

Charlotte, North Carolina, October 2017

INTRODUCTION

An interview is like a stage performance. From amateurs to the Broadway stage, performance artists wouldn't dream of crossing the stage unprepared.

An average Broadway show runs about ninety minutes, and countless hours of toil and sweat go into the performance you see unfold on stage. According to playbill.com, *"A Broadway show rehearses six days a week for eight hours a day — from around 10 AM-6 PM. The actors work for seven of those hours, and the rest is breaks. Big musicals rehearse in the studio for four to six weeks, while plays rehearse for less."*

An average interview is about thirty minutes, and while six days a week, eight hours a day would be excessive interview preparation, the point is that **preparation is the key to success.**

Remember: You won't rise to the occasion; you will rise to your level of preparation!

Intuitively, this makes sense and most would admit you shouldn't ad-lib a job interview. Yet, common knowledge is not always common practice. "Winging it" is far more common.

You might have read the job description one last time before heading to the interview. You might even have visited the company website. This expected level of preparation will not lead to a standout performance that will wow an interviewer.

This book guides you through both current best practices and surprising strategies and tactics to give you an edge in today's competitive job market.

You can use *5 Surprising Steps to Land the Job NOW!* as a reference, so feel free to flip between topics rather than reading it in order. I wrote this book for those who want to make strong impressions and leave themselves top of mind with interviewers. If you have trouble articulating your strengths, answering tricky questions, dealing with sticky situations in your background, projecting confidence, rambling, responding promptly to questions, genuinely connecting with the interviewer, or if you simply want strategies for a competitive edge, this book is for you!

The methods in the book have been tried, refined, and re-tried. At the time of this writing I have used the current process with more than two hundred people, all whom received job offers using what you're about to learn in these pages.

My hope is that you will gain new, and in many cases surprising, strategies and increased confidence to land the job you want now! So let's begin!

TIP: Download the free "Interview Prep Kit" at resources.virtuscareers.com/interview-prep-kit

STEP 1

SURPRISE! EMPLOYERS CARE ABOUT ONLY FIVE THINGS

To understand what an employer is looking for, you must think like an employer. You could be asked any of potentially hundreds of questions in an interview. However, most employers are attempting to find out <u>five</u> specific things through their questions. If you have practiced answering these five questions, you'll be far more prepared to provide what they're seeking to discover.

Employer Concern #1: Why are you here?
Why this position? Why their company? To answer this question, you must have a basic understanding of the company, what product or service it provides, who its customers are, and its culture.

Specifically, what about this opportunity excites you?

How do your values, strengths, and experience align with the job and the company?

Do your research!

- Talk to people who work or have worked at the company.
- Research the company online.

- Conduct an online news search using the company name and read any stories about the company.
- Research the company's products and services.
- Determine who this company's customers and competitors are.
- Find and note the company's vision, mission, and values.
- Locate the company's location where you will be interviewing.
- Learn about the company's history.

After reading up on the company and accessing as much information as you are able, are you more excited about the company and your chance to contribute through this role? Your feelings will show in the interview. A reason many employers pass on candidates is that they don't show passion or interest in the role.

Employer Concern #2: What can you do for us?

Do your passion, abilities, strengths, and experience meet this employer's specific needs?

Do you know what the department or company's needs are?

The job description is something you need to pay close attention to so you can proactively map what you do best to what the employer needs most. See "Step II: The Role Mapping Technique" for instructions on how to do this.

Employer Concern #3: What kind of person are you?

Do you come across as an emotionally intelligent and likable person?

Or, do you come across as someone who might be overbearing and difficult?

People hire people they like.

Are you able to concisely explain your differentiating strengths? Do you know what makes you unique? How do people describe you? Have you taken personality and strengths assessments? Can you recount solid S.T.A.R. stories that convey your best qualities? See "Step II: Storytelling with S.T.A.R." to learn more about S.T.A.R. stories.

Spend time reflecting on your qualities and strengths and ask others for feedback. Next, create short interview stories where you've demonstrated these qualities to back up your words.

Employer Concern #4: Can I afford you?

Research the market salary range for the kind of position you are seeking in your geographic location before you apply. This will help avoid wasting everyone's time if your salary expectations are way outside the range for this kind of role.

Of course, compensation is comprised of much more than base salary. Additional benefits such as paid time off, tuition reimbursement, bonuses, profit sharing, insurance, memberships, free parking, 401(k) contributions, and other perks also should be weighed.

If an interviewer asks about your salary requirements and you aren't clear about the responsibilities yet, try to delay talk about money until you gain a better understanding of the position. You could say, "I'd like to find out more about the responsibilities of the role before discussing salary."

Be prepared if they insist on knowing your expected salary in the first conversation as this is becoming standard.

To prepare, search glassdoor.com for the company to find reported salaries, and do online salary searches using job boards and sites such as salary.com for similar roles in your target area by city or zip code.

Determine the salary range for the area and position and provide the interviewer with a range, not a dollar amount. For example, "I've researched the market salary rate for similar positions in Charlotte, and the range is $75,000 to $85,000. My salary expectations are consistent with this range."

Employer Concern #5: What sets you apart from the other people we're interviewing?

The first answer to this question is that you must stand out. Are you a memorable candidate? Do you leave a strong, positive impression? The best way to distinguish yourself from other candidates is to be prepared, passionate, qualified, and positive.

Below are <u>seven</u> ways to stand out.

Seek to serve, not to get

Many candidates ask questions to discover what they'll be getting out of the employment arrangement. Seeking to serve the employer is a refreshing posture that will set you apart from other candidates.

Ask questions that demonstrate your desire to meet the needs of the employer, such as, "What is a problem you currently face that I could help you solve through this role?"

Bring an idea to the interview

After you've researched the company, further use this insight to ask about key issues and trends. Then look for opportunities to contribute ideas related to a problem they face or to make an improvement.

I recently had coffee with a woman who was one of two finalists for a position she really wanted. Despite her fit for the role and excellent qualifications, the company hired the other candidate.

The reason? The other candidate brought ideas on how to improve the company's social media presence to the interview.

Be prepared to answer the question, "What can you bring to this role?" or, "Why should we hire you?"

You need to understand your strengths, how they work together, and how they will uniquely and directly contribute to your success in the job.

While speaking about StrengthsFinder at a workshop for area job seekers, I asked for a volunteer from the audience to share his, or her, top five strengths from the assessment.

A lady shared that her strengths were Learner, Strategic, Intellection, Restorative, and WOO (Winning Others Over).

I told a quick narrative that went something like this:

When you enter a new environment or situation, you're able to get up to speed quickly on how things work (Learner), and the problems become evident to you right away (Restorative).

You're able to strategically identify only the most viable alternatives to solve those problems (Strategic), and then use your influence to implement the strategy that will solve the problem (Winning Others Over).

She looked at me and said, "That is spot on. That is what I do every day of my life at work."

An individual can often recognize his or her strengths when receiving an assessment from others, but he or she must also be able to express strengths clearly and succinctly when asked. This book delves into strengths in "Step II: List Your Assets: Create an Inventory."

Mail a handwritten thank you note

In addition to a follow-up email, write a memorable thank you note on nice card stock and send it in the mail. In your note, reference something specific the interviewer said to make a personal connection instead of a generic or clichéd note.

For example, "I was excited to hear you share about the level of collaboration required in this role. Given my experience and natural strengths of bringing people together and getting them on the same page, I'm confident I will bring this strength to your team."

BE prepared, don't just LOOK prepared

Bring articles about the company, the "About Us" page from their website, and the job description. Write on them as you do your research and put it all in a folder with the name of the department or company written prominently on the tab.

Place the folder on the table in front of you during your interview. Each time you open that folder to retrieve something, such as your resume or work samples, you'll let the interviewer know you're someone who does your homework.

Bring a work sample

This won't apply to everyone, but if the job requires creating project plans, writing proposals, designing training, architecting software, or other work you can provide, bring a sample of your work you'd be proud to leave with the interviewer. If strong written communication skills are required, bring a writing sample to demonstrate your skill. You should be prepared to leave any of your samples with the interviewer(s).

NOTE: Be extremely careful not to violate privacy or disclose trade secrets of your current or previous employer. Redact or blind sensitive information from the sample. The hiring employer will appreciate your discretion.

Build rapport with the interviewer(s). People hire people they like. Here are a few high-level rapport-building tips:

- Greet the interviewer warmly, with a firm (not *too* firm) handshake, and a smile.
- Make eye contact and say you're glad to meet the interviewer.
- Before the formal interview starts, look around the office for clues about the person such as photos, certificates, sports, or awards. Ask questions or make a comment about an object of mutual interest.
- Effective communication is comprised of only 7 percent words. The rest is your body language and tone. Use good posture, be alert but not stiff, and look interested. Walk confidently into the room, smile, and make eye contact.
- Speak clearly. Vary your pitch, pace, and tone. Slow down and emphasize important words and phrases. Talk with interest, enthusiasm, and passion.

"Step III: Savvy Rapport-Building" goes into detail about how to make a strong connection with an interviewer.

Taking time to cultivate the answers to these questions helps give the employer what they ultimately want to know. As you go through this discovery process, you might find a position or company isn't the right one for you, and that's a win, too.

STEP 2

SURPRISING PREPARATION TIPS

Social Media Strategies
Engage with the company you're targeting.

- Find out which social media outlets are most often used by your targeted companies. Most businesses commonly use Twitter, Instagram, LinkedIn, and Facebook.
- Start following target companies on social media, such as LinkedIn, Facebook, and Twitter.
- Review historical posts shared on the social media accounts.
- After doing your homework, brainstorm ways to enhance and add value to topics the company posts about.
- Regularly engage on the company's social media pages in the comments.

It is possible to become noticed with regular engagement. Companies read their social media comments, and many comments by followers are made off the cuff. Thoughtful comments will stand out!

I was having lunch with a coach colleague and friend when she told me about a client who had recently targeted Disney for his next marketing job. He used this specific strategy and was able to land a position!

The Key: You **must** add *value*. Simply stating "Great post!" does not add value when interacting with a company. One idea is to add interesting data or anecdotal evidence to support the post, share a direct experience and how you handled it or suggest an idea you have to expound upon their post.

Don't venture from your expertise and strengths. Play to your strengths when commenting. You don't know what you don't know, so stick with what you know.

Not currently targeting specific employers? Take a step back and start researching organizations who hire people for the work you do.

Engage individuals in the company.

Note: I assume in the following tips that you have a LinkedIn account. If you are new to LinkedIn, or do not have a LinkedIn account, I recommend reading Donna Serdula's book, *LinkedIn Profile Optimization for Dummies.*

In addition to company-level engagement, begin interacting with people at the companies you are targeting. For example, if you want to work in marketing at ACME Corporation, search for people on LinkedIn using search terms such as "Director of Marketing ACME." You can also visit the company's LinkedIn page to view employees who work there.

Next, view the person's profile to see if you have any connections in common who can introduce you. Then view the "Groups" section at the bottom of the person's LinkedIn profile to see what groups they belong to, join the groups of interest to you, and participate.

While you're in the person's profile, you should also look at their activity to see if they have written any posts or articles where you can add a thoughtful comment. The tip for adding value mentioned in the first social media strategy applies here, as well.

You might be saying, "I'm looking for a job in accounting, so that doesn't help me." Well, guess what? I paused when writing this and did an online search for "Top Accounting Professionals on LinkedIn" and found someone named Reg in the first result. We have three connections in common. The results are all people who live in my city. I looked at his profile and he's written five articles that I can comment on.

Next, I can send him an invitation to connect stating what I enjoyed about his article. In my invitation, I would also offer something in return such as a link to a related article in an area that he's demonstrated interest. I would also share one of his articles with my network. Every field has outspoken advocates. Find them. Interact with them. Make them your ally.

Once connected, ask for a fifteen-minute exploratory conversation to seek their opinion of working for XYZ company. While on the phone, ask if they have tips to get hired at XYZ company and then ask if you can do something in return for them. If you don't feel comfortable asking right away, wait a couple of weeks, and then ask.

Many people are using LinkedIn to ask others in their professional network for introductions to companies, so you must go an extra step and *make yourself visible* in addition to this strategy. The goal of this kind of networking is to land an exploratory interview—a short conversation that's not tied to a role but enables you to explore your interest and fit for a company.

> **TIP**: If you've applied for a position but don't have a connection in the company, used LinkedIn to follow up on the status of your application with either a recruiter or manager who works in the department you applied.

- Go to www.linkedin.com
- Enter the company name and department in the main search, such as "ACME Marketing"
- Narrow the search results to 1st and 2nd connections at the right of the webpage (see Figure 1)
- Click "shared connections" under each person in the results to see who you know in common
- You can write to the person directly, or ask your mutual connection to introduce you (preferred)
- Send a LinkedIn message to introduce yourself, state the position to which you applied, ask if they can help determine the status of your application, or know someone who could
- You can also search connections of your connections, and current and past companies of people

Figure 1

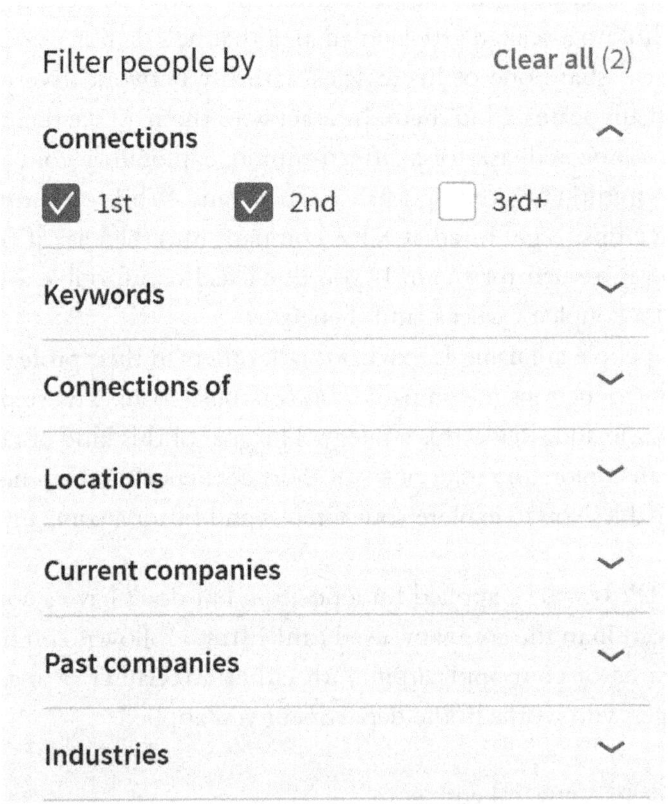

Filter people by		Clear all (2)
Connections		⌃
☑ 1st	☑ 2nd	☐ 3rd+
Keywords		⌄
Connections of		⌄
Locations		⌄
Current companies		⌄
Past companies		⌄
Industries		⌄

Once you've had an exploratory interview, you increase your chance of landing an interview for a position that might be available in the company. This is a fitting time to review the kinds of interviews you might encounter.

The Interview du Jour

Informational or Exploratory Interviews
As I mentioned in the previous section, informational/exploratory interviews are not usually tied to a position. These lead to a networking conversation that explores how you might fit into an organization. This exploration goes both ways. You are exploring the company fit, and the company is putting their feelers out to see if you are a fit for them, as well.

It's important to be able to explain the value you will bring to the company in terms of experience and strengths. This will help the person advocate for you or send you information about openings that come up in the future.

Behavioral Interviews
Behavioral interviews are among the most common for conventional occupations. The interviewer constructs their questions in a "Tell me about a time when…" or "Describe a circumstance when…" format.

The interviewer seeks to learn how you handled yourself in past situations to try to predict your performance in their organization. The interviewer is specifically interested in finding out as much as possible about your experiences, the way you tend to behave in various situations, the skills and abilities you have, how well you appear to fit the role they need to fill, and if you will fit well in their organization.

Remember to share specific examples when answering behavioral interview questions rather than speaking in general terms about yourself.

Example: "What does integrity mean to you? Tell me about a time you demonstrated integrity."

Poor answer: Integrity means doing the right thing, even if no one is looking. I pride myself on being a person of strong moral character. I have a reputation with my team as someone who is honest and ethical.

Better answer: Integrity means doing the right thing, even if no one is looking. Two weeks ago, I was working from home on a Friday when a friend called and asked me to go shopping that afternoon before my workday was over. My manager was out of town and I hadn't requested the afternoon off, so I declined my friend's request. My manager might not have known I left early, but it's important to me to make ethical choices, regardless.

Respond with S.T.A.R. stories most relevant to the question and needs of the employer. This technique is detailed in Step II. Be specific. Candidates who tell the interviewer about situations that relate to each question—rather than generalizations—are more effective. Be prepared with between three and five S.T.A.R. stories for each interview.

Phone Screen Interviews

Phone screen interviews are often the first interview you will have with a company and are always conducted over the telephone. This qualifying interview is not usually with the hiring manager, but a recruiter or other member of the company's human resources team.

At this stage, the recruiter generally seeks to eliminate candidates who do not appear to have the experience and skills necessary, are not within the salary range the company is willing to pay, or have personality or behavioral concerns that crop up during the conversation. "Step I: Employer Concern #5" discusses how to approach the salary question early in the interview process.

Manager Interview

The next interview beyond the phone screen is usually conducted by the hiring manager. The interviewer will want to go deeper into your experience and get a sense of how well you would fit into the team. The two most important outcomes from this interview are to focus on making a connection or building good rapport and to come prepared with solid examples of your accomplishments that most relate to the position.

Back-to-Back Interviews

In back-to-back interviews, you will be invited to meet with one or more individuals, one after another. For example, you might have a thirty-minute interview with your core team, then be taken to another interview with stakeholders or peers, and then another with internal customers.

Meeting with different stakeholders who will be working with you is common. You should bring a copy of your resume for each person you will be meeting. The benefit of meeting with a variety of people is it gives you a chance to ask your questions to people with different perspectives. This can give you a better picture of the role, your manager, and the team.

The Sign-off Interview

After a series of interviews, including your prospective manager and the team, you might be invited to have a final interview with your manager's boss or other senior leaders. This is more common for senior-level leadership roles to gain buy-in from the executive leadership team on your candidacy.

Panel Interviews

Panel interviews are either comprised of a mix of people you will be working with or select members of your prospective team. Pay attention to *everyone* in the room, glancing from person to person. I remember interviewing a gentleman for an instructional designer position, along with my team. After the introductions, he realized I was the manager of the people in the room and looked at me exclusively when speaking, as if my team were invisible. You bet they noticed! My team members mentioned it in the feedback they provided me, so I didn't move him to the next round.

Presentation Interviews

Presentation interviews are most common for roles where public speaking is a requirement, such as training and sales roles. Sometimes you will be provided with a presentation topic, while other times you will be expected to come up with the topic and presentation strategy on your own. Either way, it's important to know your audience. If the audience hasn't been communicated to you, it's wise to ask, otherwise you will have to respond on your feet.

Will this team appreciate humor, storytelling, or props? If you do your research on the company and the team, you'll have a better sense of the approach you should take. Is this company conservative, innovative, or fun and playful? Be careful about being too casual, but try to match the culture with your approach.

Stories are an effective way to make a memorable impression, but be sure to link your stories effectively to the stated goals of your presentation. Also, practice your presentation until you are comfortable with the content and presenting it without reading your slides. Prepare, prepare, prepare.

The Interview Before or After the Interview

Sometimes employers will ask the receptionist or others who have interacted with you about their impression of you outside of the interview. It's important to be on your best behavior from the time you pull into the parking lot until you pull out. You'd be surprised how often interviewees are reported for behavior outside the interview room, from littering to smoking in non-designated smoking areas, to talking loudly on their cell phone in reception to not being friendly to the receptionist.

Now that you have a better idea of the kinds of interviews that you might find yourself, let's take a deeper dive into how to prepare for them.

List Your Assets: Create an Inventory

The more self-awareness you possess, the better you can present yourself and explain your value to interviewers. To understand your unique contributions, explore the five areas below to discover and develop your value proposition.

Self-Reflection

Make a list of your experiences, accomplishments, awards, and successes. Think about improvements you've made, feedback, or accolades you've received. Have you mentored or developed others? Have you contributed to growth, profit, efficiency, recovered strained relationships, or obtained professional credentials?

Write keywords to describe your:

- Experiences
- Skills and Strengths
- Personality or natural behavior traits
- Interests
- Values

Experiences

Experiences include your educational background, work experience, and in some cases, personal experiences.

Skills and Strengths

Skills are the competencies that cause you to excel in a role. Your strengths are natural, or innate, abilities you possess, perhaps the ability to persuade, have empathy, or solve challenging problems). Include both your skills and strengths. Your strengths might include strategizing, mentoring, dealing with ambiguity, generating ideas, editing, writing, maintaining records, budgeting, testing, expediting, or delegating.

Personality

Your personality is defined by your natural needs, preferences, and motivations. Are you naturally organized, analytical, energetic, supportive, or decisive? Are you enthusiastic at work? Precise? Humble? Direct? Result-focused? Add these to your list of assets.

Interests

What do you like to do best? What activities do you enjoy? Do you prefer to be alone or with others? Are you most content inside or outside? Add these interests to your list.

Values

What is most important to you? Your values are key to your career satisfaction and another way to determine fit with a role and an employer. Do you value autonomy? Making a difference? Growth of yourself and others? Mastery and excellence? Reliability? Innovation? Creativity?

Would you like to discover your values? Download this values exercise from my website:

tinyurl.com/y8zy5z2j

Complete the "List Your Assets" table below using information from self-reflection, professional assessments such as StrengthsFinder, DiSC®, Myers-Briggs, Strong Inventory, Predictive Index, and feedback from others.

Input from Others

Seek feedback from people who know you well, professionally and personally. Have them answer the following questions and encourage them to be open and honest with you. Be gracious when receiving their feedback and thank them.

- What three words would you use to describe me?
- What do I do better than most others? What are my notable strengths and skills?
- What are some of my accomplishments?
- What am I passionate about, or what am I most interested in talking about?
- What character traits come to mind when you think of me?

Professional Assessments

Leverage information from any assessments you have taken such as StrengthsFinder, DiSC®, Predictive Index, WorkPlace Big Five, and Myers-Briggs Type Indicator (MBTI). I only recommend retaking an assessment if you've had major life changes, or a change in your role.

This table provides data to link your best assets to a job description in the, "Role Mapping Technique" explained below. List key career or life experiences, skills and strengths, personality traits, and interests and values from self-reflection and assessment insights by yourself, friends, and professional associates. Look for themes and key words.

List Your Assets

EXPERIENCES	SKILLS & STRENGTHS	PERSONALITY	VALUES & INTERESTS

The Clifton StrengthsFinder Assessment

In my experience as a leadership and career coach, one of the most insightful strengths assessments is the Clifton StrengthsFinder, created by the Gallup organization. It's an assessment based on a forty-year study and reveals the thirty-four most common talents in people. You can access this assessment at www.gallupstrengthscenter.com.

Why do strengths matter?

According to Gallup, one in thirty-three million people share the same top five strengths. This means it's unlikely anyone on the team, or even the company, you're seeking to join will share your strengths. The other candidates interviewing definitely will not share your strengths. This positions you to bring unique contributions that come easily for you.

Demonstrating awareness of your strengths and effectively explaining them to a prospective employer is compelling and powerful.

In addition, working within one's natural talents increases productivity and quality and decreases stress. If you know your strengths, you can target roles that will use them. Awareness of your natural talents equips you to be intentional in using them every day. When you play to your strengths, your work becomes more energizing.

Where do your strengths lie?

Your strengths are not the same as your transferable skills, so when you're exploring your strengths, you don't want to list job skills. Again, your strengths are your unique natural talents, not the ability to create pivot tables in Excel.

In addition to knowing your specific strengths, you can learn the themes of your strengths. StrengthsFinder identifies four categories, or themes, for the thirty-four strengths:

> *Relating* – Explains how you build connections with other people (people-facing strengths)
> *Influencing* – Details how you motivate others to action (people-facing strengths)
> *Executing* – Clarifies what drives you toward results; these individuals are doers (inward-facing strengths)
> *Thinking* – Reveals how you analyze the world (inward-facing strengths)

Knowing where your strengths lie not only reveals your advantages, which you should leverage and develop, this knowledge also highlights blind spots, which enables you to target strengths you can use to compensate. I do this all the time. Most of my strengths are Thinking themes: Strategic, Ideation, Futuristic, and Input.

I can't connect with people or build relationships if I live in my own head, which is the tendency of people with Thinking themes. To avoid this, I rely heavily on my Influencing theme: Maximizer.

StrengthsFinder advises people with Maximizer to "Seek roles in which you are helping other people succeed. In coaching, managing, mentoring, or teaching roles, your focus on strengths will prove particularly beneficial to others." My desire to help people succeed draws me out of my own head.

A client told me that during a recent interview she was asked what words she would use to describe herself. How convenient! I had created a one-page summary of her strengths based on the assessments she's done. She pulled it out and summarized her results for them:

> I do the right thing. I do things right, and I do what I say I'm going to do. (Responsibility)
> I'm a problem solver, troubleshooter, and I find improvements and solutions. (Restorative)
> I'm always learning, and I catch on quickly. (Learner)
> I grow talent in others and enjoy helping others succeed. (Developer)
> I'm a negotiator who sees both sides of a situation, enabling me to arrive at consensus. (Harmony)
> You can bet the employer was impressed!

I have my top five strengths. Now what?

First, become intimately acquainted with your strengths.

The true value of your strengths is the interpretation. Too many people take the assessment, read their strengths, and place the report in a drawer. They miss a tremendous opportunity. Transformation comes through the powerful narrative of knowing who you are and how you operate.

I have a client whose top strength is Communication, and her next two strengths are Discipline and WOO (Winning Others Over). I explained to her that when WOO (natural networker) and Communication (natural storyteller) are working together, she's the life of the party—she's networking, making friends, and building connections.

However, when Discipline (creates structure) and Communication (natural storyteller) are working together, she is communicating policy, standards, and ensuring people are following guidelines. One of those presentations of her personality is task-oriented (Communication + Discipline), while the other is relationship oriented (Communication + WOO).

Understanding how she's perceived has enhanced her emotional intelligence and increased awareness of her effect on co-workers, who might be confused by shifts between the two personas. This kind of insight can greatly impact your life.

A client recently had a job interview with a large pharmaceutical manufacturer. She did not meet requirements for the position, but they were so impressed by her Learner strength that they offered her the job in the interview.

Next, ask yourself some questions:

- How do your strengths align with the role and related job description?
- What are some ways your strengths are unique in how you approach your work?
- How have you performed better than your peers because of your strengths?
- Are you able to identify potential gaps between critical strengths a role requires and your strengths?
- How might you leverage your other strengths to meet those gaps?

Work your strengths into your networking conversations (previously called an elevator pitch), interview answers, cover letters, LinkedIn profile, and your resume.

Discussing your strengths is a language, so the more you practice, the more fluent you'll become telling your strengths story in interviews.

If you're not familiar with effective interview storytelling strategies or struggle to easily answer interview questions, the next section is for you.

Storytelling with S.T.A.R.

As a hiring manager, I was surprised how often people answered a specific behavior-based question with a general response. For example, when I was an operations manager interviewing for an open role on my team, I asked, "What does integrity mean to you? And tell me about a time you demonstrated integrity at work."

The candidate proceeded to share that integrity is doing the right thing, even when no one is looking (so far, so good), but then she continued sharing a general self-assessment about her commitment to always do the right thing and go above and beyond. Nowhere in her answer did she share a <u>specific</u> example of when she demonstrated integrity on the job.

When asked a behavior-based question, remember to avoid present tense generalizations such as, "I always..." Talk is cheap, and anyone can say what an interviewer wants to hear or what they think they would do in a theoretical situation. The hiring manager wants to hear what you did in a real situation. Prove it with the S.T.A.R. format!

S.T.A.R. is an acronym for **S**ituation, **T**ask, **A**ction, and **R**esult. S.T.A.R. stories are used to answer behavior-based questions that begin, Tell me about a time when..."

Situation

What was the problem or opportunity you faced? Provide a *brief* background. I can't emphasize enough the importance of brevity! You might be tempted to share every detail. Please don't!

An interviewer needs only enough context to grasp and understand the significance of the RESULT. The result is the most important part of your story, yet many interviewees begin rambling about the situation and sharing unnecessary details the employer cares little about.

Task

How did you address the problem or opportunity you faced? In other words, what was the end goal? Again, keep this brief.

Action

What specific actions did you take? What was your involvement? How did you contribute? In short, what did you do? Don't dig into the gory details of every step. What label can you give what you did to convey meaning without a lengthy explanation of all the steps?

For example, "I performed a root cause analysis" or "I developed a detailed project plan" conveys a lot of meaning, which eliminates the need to describe each step you performed in detail.

Result

The result is the outcome of your action and the most important part of the story. How did you make a difference? Did you save the company time, money, or other resources? Did someone get a promotion because of your investment in them? Did you increase efficiencies? Did you do something that hadn't been thought of or tried before?

Providing context of why the result mattered is important. Interviewers don't know why your outcome is a big deal, so you'll need to help them understand. Let's look at an example.

> *Employer:* What is an accomplishment you're proud of?
>
> *Interviewee:* Last year I was selected to join the company's leadership development program.

As an interviewer, my first question is, so what? This is not a high impact statement because no context is provided.

Was this program exclusive, or are 90 percent of employees given the same opportunity? How many others were selected? Out of how many? Did you have to be nominated, versus applying for yourself?

Let's look at a more effective response.

> *Interviewee:* Recently, I was nominated by a senior leader in the company to participate in a high potential leadership program. Two-hundred sixty-four employees were nominated, and I was one of only five people selected.

Here's another example:

> *Interviewer:* Tell me about a recent success.
>
> *Interviewee:* Last year I managed a shared services integration project with a positive process and financial outcome.

This is an actual example from a client. Were they selected for the project? Was it enterprise-wide, or a small project? How complex was the project? Was it a high visibility project?

Sometimes you might not have numbers if you didn't take them with you from your last job. It's okay if you don't have them. You can characterize your success using words. Let's look at where this accomplishment ended up after I asked my client these questions.

> *Interviewee:* I was appointed as the program manager to oversee five project managers on a highly confidential, business-critical shared services integration for a Fortune 100 company, which finished on time and within budget and resulted in a stronger financial position for the company.

Context. Context. Context! An accomplishment might not seem like a big deal to you, but don't assume it won't be to someone else.

S.T.A.R. story sources
Remembering specific stories over the course of your career can be difficult, so this list should help you derive a variety of sources to create your stories.

Job Descriptions

The most important source of inspiration for interview stories is the company's own job description for the position. Reading what they are looking for in the position description should prompt you to think of, and capture, situations when you've accomplished what they are describing.

Your Strengths

You perform at your best when using your natural talents. Once you've taken StrengthsFinder, take time to read and learn your results and generate examples that showcase the strengths. If you log into www. gallupstrengthscenter.com using the credentials you created to take the assessment you can download the Strengths Insight Guide report, which is full of adjectives you can use to convey your strengths through stories.

Underline key phrases that describe you and put yourself in the scene at work to remember situations when you've used the strength.

Employer Values

Values based decision-making is becoming more common. Your values are your determination of what's most important to you. If you know what's most important to employers, that insight enables you to reflect on situations when you've demonstrated the values they seek and turn those experiences into S.T.A.R. stories.

Any chance you get, weave your values into the stories you plan to tell so you demonstrate not only results but also these values. When employers are surveyed about the work values they consider most important in employees, these ten top the list.:

Strong Work Ethic – Do you often go the extra mile and do more than expected? Think of times you've added value with your strong work ethic and achievement orientation. This will give the employer a sense of what to expect if they hire you.

Dependability and Responsibility – Do you always meet your deadlines, show up on time, do what you say you're going to do, or take accountability for your actions and behavior? Weave accountability and reliability into your answers.

Possessing a Positive Attitude – Are you someone who moves beyond the challenges that inevitably come up in any job? Do you create an environment of good will and behave as a good role model for others? If your interview stories convey this tendency, you will help the employer see the valuable impact you will have on their workplace culture.

Adaptability – Are you open to change and improvements? Employees sometimes complain that changes in the workplace don't make sense or make their work harder; oftentimes these complaints are due to a lack of flexibility. Demonstrate your valuable trait of flexibility. Few want to work with inflexible people.

Honesty and Integrity – Are you trustworthy? Ensure your employer can trust what you say and what you do.

Self-Motivated – Are you a self-starter? After you understand your responsibility on the job, do it without any prodding from others.

Motivated to Grow and Learn – Does your resume demonstrate you seek growth? Employers want employees who are interested in keeping up with new developments and knowledge in the field. One of the top reasons employees leave their employers is the lack of opportunity for career development within the organization.

Confidence – Do you convey self-assurance without arrogance? Confident people do not feel the need to impress others with what they know because they feel comfortable with themselves and don't believe they need to know everything. Confident people admit mistakes.

Professionalism – Do you look and act the part? Professional behavior includes learning every aspect of a job and doing it to the best of one's ability. Professionals look, speak, and dress accordingly to maintain an image of someone who takes pride in their behavior and appearance.

Loyalty – Do you project a desire to be a devoted worker? Demonstrate how you foster good relationships based on loyalty.

Performance Reviews and Feedback

In my experience, managers don't always write robust, fact-based performance reviews. By the time performance review rolls around, unless they've kept records and notes about you, your performance review could reflect opinions and impressions rather than observed behavior.

Therefore, you are responsible for documenting accomplishments and feedback about your performance. My colleague, Dave, keeps an "I Love Me" binder that contains formal performance reviews and awards he's received throughout his career.

If you haven't been keeping these details, don't worry, you can start now. A Chinese proverb says the best time to plant a tree was twenty years ago, but the second-best time is now.

When I worked in the corporate world, I kept a kudos folder to store feedback, reviews, emails, ideas or improvements I implemented, and other proof of performance. If you receive positive comments in emails, print them or save them where they won't be lost, such as in the cloud or on a memory stick.

Do not store your kudos folder on your work computer! If you're ever let go unexpectedly, you probably won't be given a chance to retrieve anything other than your personal effects from your work area.

Therefore, keep your kudos in your personal computer, but make sure it's backed up in the cloud or on a memory stick so you don't lose everything in the event of a hard drive crash.

Career Accomplishments and Results
Think about the outcomes and results you've given your employers. Ideally you're tracking your process improvements, new processes, people you've mentored or coached to promotion, etc., and can access these to create stories. If you haven't been keeping track, start now.

The Role Mapping Technique

If you do only one thing to prepare for an interview, this technique should be it. The role mapping technique aligns you, item by item, with a job description, and I'm going to show you exactly how to do it. The free "Interview Prep Kit" included with this book contains the Role Mapping Worksheet and other resources to help you be prepared. Download at resources.virtuscareers.com/interview-prep-kit.

Once you locate a job posting you're interested in applying for, save the job description to your computer. If the job is posted online, take your mouse and highlight the text of the job description, copy and paste it into your word processing program, and save it with the company name and job title. Why do this? When you apply for a job, you want to access the job description after it is taken down.

Go over the job description you've copied and saved, then highlight key words and phrases that tell what the company is seeking in a candidate: skills, experiences, personality, character traits, etc.

Next follow these steps (An example is shown in the table below.):

- List **requirements** you highlighted for the targeted position in the *Employer Need* column.
- List the **experiences/skills, personality traits, strengths and values** (see the "List Your Assets: Create an Inventory" section) related to the requirements under *What I Do Best*.

- Write a **story** illustrating proof of what you do best under *Tell My Story* as pre-work for an interview. What did you do? What difference did it make? Use the S.T.A.R. format (**S**ituation, **T**ask, **A**ction, **R**esult.

Role Mapping

EMPLOYER NEED	WHAT I DO BEST	TELL MY STORY
Improve systems, processes, policies	-Improved 12 processes in current role in the past year	I have improved processes in every role in the past 10 years. In my current position, I have made 12 process improvements in the past year, including moving from a manual spreadsheet process for our client pricing to a web-based system, which has increased my team's profitability by 25%.
Long-term planning	-4 years' strategic planning exp. at ACME. -Strategic thinking is a top five strength in StrengthsFinder.	In my current role as an operations manager, I have been directly involved in program strategic planning for three consecutive years. The annual planning process includes program growth strategy, associate learning and development strategy, customer experience and retention strategy, and business process innovation. We have experienced financial growth year-over-year, as well as low employee turnover of less than 5%. In addition, we have seen 15% growth of our new customer base, and a 25% increase in existing customer sales.
Payroll management	No experience	While I have not had direct experience w/payroll, I have Learner in my top five strengths, which means I learn new things very quickly. For example, I managed a $3M budgetary process independently within two weeks with no prior budgeting experience.

By completing this role mapping exercise, you will be equipped and prepared with solid stories linked directly to the requirements of the role. Now, let's review some surprising and unconventional ways to enhance your interview performance!

Brain-based Success Tips

Ha! Ha! Ha!

Before you go into your interview watch YouTube videos of things that make you laugh such as crazy cat videos, babies laughing hysterically, or whatever tickles your funny bone.

When you laugh, your brain releases chemicals called endorphins. One of laughter's many benefits is presenting a more relaxed and positive demeanor, which people find appealing.

Nom. Nom.
Eat ⅛ cup of almonds an hour before your interview. Almonds have magnesium, which increases the development of serotonin, contributing to feeling happy and balancing your mood.

Happy people are also more attractive.

"Gratitude is the sign of a noble soul."

– Aesop

Did you know gratitude makes others like us more? People with 10 percent more gratitude than average have 17.5 percent more social capital.

Start making a daily list of things you're grateful for (Nothing is too small!), and it will shape your personality and what you project to others.

Before heading into your interview, list three good things that happened in your week, or three things you are thankful for. Try not to repeat the same things each time, as we tend to become desensitized by repetition.

V for Victory!
Before your interview, head to the bathroom and stand in a victory pose (arms up in a "V" overhead) for two solid minutes. I prefer the Wonder Woman™ pose, personally. Power poses release testosterone, which increases confidence, decreases cortisol, and reduces stress.

Confidence—that happy place between self-doubt and arrogance—is an attractive quality. I recommend watching Amy Cuddy's popular Ted Talk on YouTube titled, *Your Body Language May Shape Who You Are.*

You can combine the four tips above with the conventional interview preparation techniques below to prime your brain and create better chemistry with interviewers. If you'd like to also leverage personality to make an even stronger connection, see "Step III: Savvy Rapport-Building."

Interview Preparation Tips

I will emphasize the importance of preparedness repeatedly through this book. Here are additional interview preparation tips to ensure peak interview performance.

- Research the team, what they do, and the roles within their department.
- Call contacts you might have to ask about the company, the team, and about key issues and trends.
- Make a list of questions to ask, points to make, and S.T.A.R. stories to share during your interview.
- Work through practice questions with a friend or co-worker and get honest feedback.
- Be sure you know the interview location. Take a test run beforehand to find it, if needed.
- Eat right and get plenty of rest the day before the interview.
- Clean out your car. The interview starts when you arrive in the parking lot.
- Dress for success. Look your best, conservatively. Wear little or no jewelry, except for a watch, wedding ring, and (for women) conservative earrings. You want to look professional so the focus will be on what you have to say and not how you look.
- Do not wear cologne, perfume, or other scents. Interviewers might be sensitive or not like your scent choice, which could leave a negative impression.
- If you need a haircut, get one.

Introvert Interview Tips

In 2016, I delivered a keynote address to a group of Human Resources and Career Services Professionals at the Career Thought Leaders conference in Denver, Colorado.

Author Chris Guillebeau was also asked to speak at the event to discuss his most recent book, *Born for This*. When Chris began speaking, the audience quickly realized he was not your typical inspirational, larger-than-life speaker. In fact, he was soft-spoken and introverted. Because Chris was so unassuming, I was intrigued to see, and somewhat concerned how, he was going to capture the attention of the audience.

His talk was one of the most interesting and thought-provoking I had heard, despite a lack of grand hand gestures and a gregarious manner of speaking. The audience seemed to hang on each word he said. His ability to tell stories, authentic presentation style, and subtle use of wit were a winning trifecta that held the crowd's attention.

If you're an introvert, what are positive and attractive qualities YOU possess? Rather than believing you must turn on the charm of an extrovert to win over an interviewer, write down a list of some of your best qualities, as discussed in "List Your Assets: Create an Inventory."

Focus on showcasing your talents. Are you skilled at explaining complex concepts simply? Make sure you include a S.T.A.R. story that displays this ability.

Take advantage of your reserved and quantitative nature. You can prepare and present your accomplishments objectively without coming across as boastful. Your reserved tendencies lend well to sharing data-driven facts about your successes, humbly.

To build rapport, think of comments and questions you can make or ask in advance to help break the ice and get the other person talking. For example, as you're shaking hands and shown to your seat you could say, "It's nice to meet you and I appreciate being invited here today. I saw on LinkedIn you've been here ten years. What do you like best about working here?"

In general, when you ask thoughtful questions and listen well, people consider you a skilled conversationalist. As you're leaving, you can comment on or thank the interviewer for something you appreciated about the interview process or some detail you noticed while there.

Remember to smile when meeting the interviewer and when parting ways. If they make a humorous comment during the interview and they are smiling, return the smile and perhaps a subtle head nod to acknowledge their humor.

Flip the Interview

I've read a lot of advice regarding questions to ask an interviewer. Some questions are suggested to make you look smart or impress the interviewer. "What is your five-year plan to stay ahead in the competitive IoT (Internet of Things) landscape?" No, no, no!

Unless this is directly relevant to your role and responsibilities, don't do it. Here's why:

- What if the interviewer doesn't know the answer to your question? Embarrassing an interviewer by making them look ignorant is not a winning strategy and will not earn you any points.
- Does the answer to this question influence whether you'll accept an offer? I recommend you ask only questions that help you decide you want the job.

I also don't recommend asking questions of a hiring manager in an interview that you could find through other sources, such as the company website or human resources. For example: What are your main products? What are your hours of operation? Who are your biggest competitors?

Finally, I would avoid questions early in the interview process that should be reserved for when you are a finalist. For example, questions about benefits, flexible working arrangements, and remote work are not appropriate in a first interview.

When I was a hiring manager, a woman asked me in an initial phone screen, I have some health problems, so I need good health insurance. What are the medical benefits like? Not only is such personal information best avoided in an interview, the screening interview is way too premature to discuss benefits.

So, what should you ask an employer? Ask questions that are *employer-centric* wherever possible so you aren't singing the *All About Me* song. If you ask a string of questions centered around yourself (When am I eligible for a promotion? What kind of training will I get? Will I get an office or a cube?), you will come across as self-interested.

Here are some sample questions you might ask:

- Why is this role currently vacant?
- Why did you choose to work here, and what keeps you here?
- What can you tell me about the leadership style in this department?
- What is a problem you're facing that I might help you solve through this position?
- How will you measure my performance? What will have happened six months from now that will demonstrate I've met your expectations?
- Now that we've talked about my qualifications and the job, do you have any concerns about me succeeding in this position?
- What is our next step?

TIP: Download the free "Interview Prep Kit" at resources.virtuscareers.com/interview-prep-kit for questions to ask the hiring manager so you can determine their supervisory and leadership style.

In addition to informational questions, you can use questions as a strategy to demonstrate your knowledge or expertise. For example, the last interview I had was to lead the Learning and Development function.

During the interview, to demonstrate my strengths, I asked my soon-to-be manager if she'd ever heard of the StrengthsFinder assessment, and she had. I used the question as a segue to explain my top five strengths to her and how they would align with the needs outlined in the job description.

What to Bring

- Something that makes you stand out and leaves an impression. A one-page summary of your strengths, work samples, and your brag book are excellent resources.
- Writing pad and pen for note-taking.
- Extra copies of your resume for each person you'll meet, a couple of spares, and one for yourself.
- Information about the job in a folder with the team or position name on the tab.
- A list of your questions, points you want to make, and S.T.A.R. stories to tell.

STEP 3

SURPRISING PERFORMANCE TIPS

It's Show Time!

- Arrive at least five minutes before the interview.
- Be friendly to everyone. People might not be interviewing you, but they will be making observations.
- Greet the interviewer with a warm smile and a firm handshake.
- Look them in the eyes and tell them how glad you are to meet with them.
- Effective communication is only 7 percent words. The other 93 percent is tone and body language, or how you carry yourself. Sit up with interest. Stand straight but not stiff. Walk with purpose. Smile with confidence.
- Look around the office for clues about the person such as photos, certificates, or awards.
- Ask questions or comment on objects of mutual interest.
- Listen closely to what is being said.
- Observe the interviewer and match their style and pace.
- Speak clearly with enough volume to be heard. Vary your pitch and pace. Slow down and emphasize important words and phrases.

How you say what you say is as important as the words you deliver. Talk with interest, enthusiasm, and passion.

- Answer the interviewer's questions confidently and honestly. Look for opportunities to share relevant S.T.A.R. stories.
- Limit answers from twenty seconds to no more than two minutes. The interviewer will ask for more if they're interested.
- Feel free to pause to arrange your thoughts. If you do not understand a question, ask for clarification.
- Attitude is key to your success. Don't be cocky. Confidence is good. Overconfidence is not.
- Always be positive in your answers. Never say anything negative.
- As the interviewer describes the job, ask questions about the role and the work. Seek to understand what needs to be accomplished through the job. You might ask what they are looking for in the successful candidate.
- Take notes.
- Thank the interviewer at the close of the interview.
- Tell them you enjoyed the interview and learning about the position. Then ask about next steps and timing.
- Send a thank you note in the mail, as well as an email.
- Be forthcoming if you would like to move to the next step. If you are interested in the position, say so. If not, do not.
- Do not burn bridges with anyone, whatever the situation.

Savvy Rapport-Building

People-reading and adapting to the person you are communicating with can result in improved interpersonal success, particularly in a job interview.

I'm not suggesting you act inauthentic, fake, or phony. Simply focus on the needs of the person on the other side of the table. As an example, if your interviewer is talkative, and you're also a talker, practice listening and allow your interviewer to do most of the talking. This isn't changing who you are, it's displaying flexible behavior based on the person you're interacting with.

Learning to read people isn't difficult, and it can provide a significant professional advantage. Reading people requires only three things: identification, observation, and practice.

As a human behavior consultant and career coach, I frequently have conversations with my clients and end up coaching them about an interpersonal conflict. In fact, personal interaction often drives clients to seek my services. Learning to read and manage different personalities has been instrumental in virtually eliminating my own conflict with others.

Many models describe personality, yet the DISC® personality profile is one of the most common. I'll use this model to cover three key points:

- The characteristics of the four personality styles
- How to identify a person's personality style
- Simple techniques to improve communication with each style

The Four Personality Characteristics: DiSC®
Let's spend a few minutes looking at how this model explains the characteristics, needs, and motivations of people through four personality styles.

Dominance (D)

Dominance, or D, denotes a strong personality. These task-oriented, decisive people focus on challenging themselves and others, getting results and taking action. They prefer the big picture. They are also fast-paced multi-taskers. Ds are often verbal, take-charge people.

Ds enjoy leading others; many leaders are primary or secondary *D's*. This style thrives in fast-paced environments where people value action, results, and challenging the status quo. Two-thirds of leaders in the corporate environment have dominance as a primary or secondary personality style. Steve Jobs was Dominance-driven, and so are Donald Trump and Hillary Clinton.

Influence (I)

Influence, or *I* personalities, are also big picture, fast-paced, multi-tasking, and verbal. The core difference between Influencing and Dominant people is that *I's* are relationship-oriented, not task-oriented. *I's* are enthusiastic, energetic, and inspirational. They want to be liked and appreciate recognition.

   I's are enthusiastic, enjoy working with a variety of different people, and are satisfied when their jobs provide recognition and reward, variety, and the opportunity to manage relationships and influence others. *I's* often gravitate to fields based on working with people and are comfortable in sales, training, speaking, consulting, or performing. Oprah Winfrey is an *I*, and so was Robin Williams.

Steady (S)

Steady, or *S*, is similar to *I* in being relationship-oriented. They differ from *I's* in being calmer and less verbal. Steady personalities are opposite of *D's*. *S's* work in a linear mode at a more moderate pace. They are loyal, good listeners who express warmth and friendliness.

   S's like working with a team and building authentic, strong, and supportive work relationships. They value support, stability, and collaboration. They gravitate to roles such as teaching, counseling, administrative support, or social work. Their work style is methodical and detail-oriented; they do not prefer to multi-task. *S's* often seek work helping others, such as jobs in the non-profit sector, education, ministry, and healthcare. Mother Teresa and Mr. Rogers were *S's*.

Conscientiousness (C)

Conscientious, or *C's*, are detail-oriented, (versus big picture *D's* and *I's*). *C's* have a reserved temperament. They are process-oriented and value stability. However, *C's* differ from *S's* in that they are task-oriented, rather than relationship-oriented.

C's enjoy work that requires attention to detail, quality, accuracy, and logic. Because they are task-oriented, *C's* are often found in technology, engineering, quality, and compliance. Bill Gates is a *C*. So was Albert Einstein.

Interactions between DiSC® Styles

Eighty-five percent of people have a blend of two personality styles; only 15 percent of the population has one style. A person with a secondary trait will have a different personality than another person with the same singular primary trait.

Have you noticed the similarities between individual styles? Often a priority straddles two quadrants of the circle (Figure 2a). The overlap between styles creates common ground:

> *D's* and *I's* prioritize *action.*
> *I's* and *S's* prioritize *collaboration.*
> *C's* and *S's* prioritize *stability.*
> *D's* and *C's* prioritize *challenge.*

D's and *S's* do not share common priorities, nor do *I's* and *C's*. These personality combinations may be prone to greater friction and have more difficulty understanding each other.

Figure 2a

Attributes of the Styles

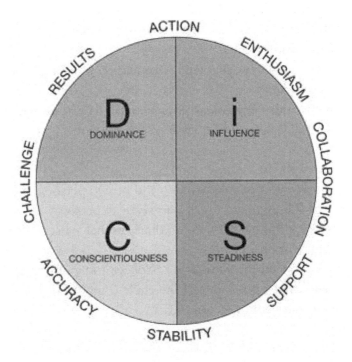

What's your interviewer's DiSC® style?

Let me share a technique that will help you identify an interviewer's style.

1. Are *they fast-paced and outspoken* **OR** *cautious and reflective?*
2. Are *they questioning and skeptical* **OR** *accepting and warm?*
3. Combine your answers to questions 1 and 2 to discover their style. For example, if you said *fast-paced and outspoken + accepting and warm,* their primary style is *I.*

Figure 2b

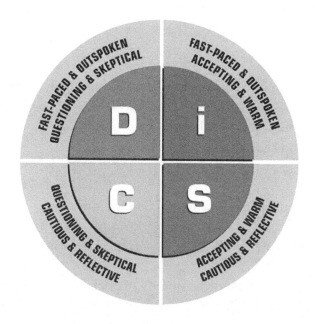

D's and *C's* are task-oriented, while *I's* and *S's* are relationship-oriented. *D's* and *I's* are fast-paced, big picture thinkers. *C's* and *S's* are detail-oriented and like to work at a moderate pace.

Learning to Read People
Three main cues help you identify personality in your interview: facial expression, hand gestures, and verbal cues. If your interview is over the phone, you'll need to focus on verbal cues.

Facial Expression
When talking to someone, how much do they smile?

- Lots of smiles = I or S
- Only socially required smiles = D or C (perhaps when being introduced)

Hand Gestures
How animated are the person's hand gestures and body movement?

- Slow and close to body = C or S
- Fast and away from body = D or I

Verbal Cues
How fast does the person speak, and do they interrupt?

- Speaks more slowly and will stop speaking when interrupted = C or S
- Fast-paced speaker who doesn't stop when interrupted = D or I

How much small talk?

- Makes small talk (perhaps talks about personal life) = I or S
- Sticks to task and work topics = D or C

Q: How can you tell if a person who smiles a lot is an I or S?
A: Look at the hand gestures. Slow/close to body is an S. Fast and away from body is an I.

Q: How can you tell if a person who talks fast and interrupts is a D or I?
A: If they are usually engaging in small talk and smiling, they are an I. If they stick to task-related topics and are not smiling profusely, they are a D.

Rapport-Building Techniques

When Communicating with a Dominant (D) Personality

DO	LIMIT THESE
Be clear and to the point	Appearing overly friendly
Focus on your results	Making generalizations
Start with the bottom line	Talking too much
Keep on the big picture	Repeating yourself
Stick to the subject	Making unsupportable statements
Be logical in presenting facts	Getting emotional
Ask pertinent questions	Behaving in a loud or boisterous way
Remember: Relationship is secondary to tasks	Going off on tangents

When Communicating with an Influential (I) Personality

DO	LIMIT THESE
Be open, warm, and friendly	Restricting their time
Concentrate on the people aspect	Showing a "cold" manner
Take time, socialize	Doing all the talking
Show enthusiasm	Being abrupt
Listen attentively	Restricting their ideas/suggestions
Emphasize your collaborative efforts	Looking at your watch

When Communicating with an Steady (S) Personality

DO	LIMIT THESE
Be sincere	Overpowering
Demonstrate warmth	Demanding or dominating
Ask questions, listen	Pushing ideas too aggressively
Show interest in them and their work	Stating too many facts
Take an easy-going approach	Asking closed-ended (yes/no) questions
Smile!	Making communication one-way
Focus on accomplishments that create stability	Making "casual" promises

When Communicating with a Conscientious (C) Personality

DO	LIMIT THESE
Be organized	Generalizing details
Think "professional" for presentations	Appearing vague
Focus on quality and accuracy of your results	Acting too casual
Concentrate on specifics (the "how")	Wasting time on casual conversation
Talk to them about objective, fact-based aspects of ideas and past projects	Jumping around from one point to another
Stick with logic and facts	Acting too familiar
Avoid pressuring them for an immediate decision	Assuming they will trust quickly

Using personality identification tips should help you better connect and communicate with different styles and enhance rapport with interviewers. Because in recognizing their styles, you allow them to set the pace and tone of the interview and then follow their lead.

What Every "Body" is Saying

You can learn a lot about interviewers by observing their body posture and gestures, and an interviewer can also learn a lot about you, because fifty-five percent of communication is body language.

When I was a hiring manager, I tried to be conscious of my body language in interviews, and I watched closely the gestures of those I interviewed.

We learn to control and mask our facial cues more than any other part of our body, so the most unmasked, truthful body language is observed at the extremities.

Below are some body language considerations to note while interviewing.

Feet and legs

When someone turns their feet away from you, either both feet, or with one foot turned away creating an "L" formation, this means they are ready to depart the conversation. They may even swivel their chair so their lower body and torso is pointed away from you.

Alternatively, when a person's feet (and torso) directly face you, this is a sign of engagement. Keep your feet pointed directly at the interviewer.

When a person has crossed legs and begins bouncing their upper foot, this can be a sign of discomfort or lack of interest.

If you notice someone disengaging from the conversation with their legs and feet, check your body to ensure you're not initiating their discomfort with your non-verbal gestures. After the interview, perhaps you can determine what you were saying when you noticed a change in their body language.

Watch what your feet and legs convey.

Keep your ankles *uncrossed* if your legs are directly in front of you. Crossed ankles suggest insecurity or discomfort. I've seen many interviewees do this.

Jiggling your legs projects nervousness and anxiety.

Upper body

People tend to lean back and away from someone in an interview when not connecting. However, this can also be a territorial posture when coupled with splayed legs (usually in men). Conversely, we lean into people when we are comfortable with them. Leaning forward slightly is preferable to leaning back or sitting stiffly, as it displays approachability and comfort with the interviewer.

Arm crossing is a protective gesture. When someone blocks their upper body with crossed arms, it's an indication they're being guarded when interacting with you. Gripping crossed arms with fingers is an elevated sign of discomfort. Do not cross your arms in an interview; it makes you appear closed off, defensive, or insecure.

Don't allow your shoulders to rise. Keep them pulled down and slightly pulled back in proper posture. Shrugged or slumped shoulders displays lack of confidence.

Hand gestures

When an interviewer is leaning in toward you and has interlocked fingers with thumbs pointing upward, this is a comfortable, open, conversational position. Watch for hands in pockets, especially if the person is leaning back in their chair. This is a dismissive posture.

To re-engage the interviewer, try to determine if you might be doing something to put them off. Are you talking too much? Are your answers too long? Are you being negative? Are you keeping up with the pace of the interviewers? Continue to be friendly, but not over-friendly, and smile.

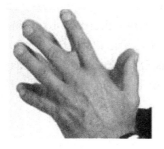

People tend to wring their hands, or rub their palms together when they are nervous. Pay attention to how you use your hands. The interviewer will notice.

Women are especially prone to touching their hair in an interview, whether pushing away their bangs or tucking hair behind their ears. This is distracting and comes across as unprofessional. Consider wearing your hair in a style that reduces the chance you'll touch it if you have this habit.

Another hand consideration is to avoid wiping yours after shaking hands with the interviewer, either with your other hand or on the side of your pant leg or skirt.

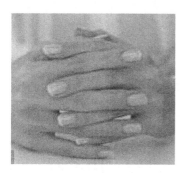

One of the most confident hand positions is steepled hands, finger-tip to finger-tip. You can have them steepled on your lap, or resting on the table in front of you. Try not to appear wooden. You have no need to keep your hands in one position the entire interview. Avoid keeping your hands concealed, such as under the table, and avoid tapping or fidgeting your fingers.

Loosely interlocked fingers are a comfortable alternative if you aren't quite ready for steepled fingers.

Facial cues
Some negative facial non-verbal cues include:

- Furrowed eye brows
- Tightly pursed lips, with or without the corners of the mouth down-turned
- Squinting
- A delay in opening the eyes after closing them
- Polite smiles where the corners of the mouth move out toward the ears, instead of curving up toward the eyes

Watch your own facial cues to ensure you're not projecting these negative non-verbals. In addition, avoid licking your bottom lip. If you're nervous, you might do this to soothe yourself unconsciously.

When you smile, ensure the corners of your mouth are upturned, exposing your teeth. Smiles with closed lips often appear forced.

A slight head tilt also is a positive sign. Individuals convey openness and receptivity with this gesture. They don't tend to head tilt unless they like you.

If you choose to practice a mock interview with a friend or coach, take some video footage with your smart phone to see if you're talking too fast and unconsciously creating distractions, or if your body language is sending a positive message.

Handling Difficult Questions
One thing people dread about interviews is they anticipate questions they aren't comfortable answering or aren't sure how to handle. Following are a few of the questions people often struggle with.

What is your greatest weakness?
Most interviewers ask this question for one or more of these reasons:

> *Looking for red flags* – Some interviewers are looking for personality flaws and other traits that could cause them not to want to work with you.
> *Determining your capacity to grow as a person* – Are you someone who seeks to grow, or do you accept your weaknesses and expect everyone else to, as well? I am not a proponent of

investing time and energy on weaknesses. However, if you have a weakness that is a possible career-killer, hiring managers must understand you're willing to grow as a person. *Gauging your self-awareness* – Knowing your weaknesses demonstrates you're aware of, and have accepted, your shortcomings. No one wants to work with someone who thinks they're perfect.

Avoid answering this question as a humble brag such as, "I'm a perfectionist," or "I work too much."

Share a true weakness that is not key to the role, but not completely unrelated to it. Avoid interpersonal weaknesses unless you can demonstrate great improvement. Keep it brief. Do not elaborate. Shift immediately to share what you have learned or done to improve. An even better option is to share feedback you received about a weakness that you subsequently acted upon to improve, because it shows you are coachable.

Tell me about yourself

If asked, "Tell me about yourself" in an interview, how would you answer? Most people I talk to really dread this question.

I've interviewed many hundreds of people, and almost always the response is a synopsis of work history or some variant of their resume. *This is the wrong answer.*

You're not adding value or setting yourself apart from the competition by regurgitating information that a hiring manager is already holding in their hand. Consider tackling this with an entirely different approach. (But before you do, you'll need to do your homework).

Do you know the pain you solve, how you solve it with your skills and strengths, and the value you provide an employer as a result? You are more than a list of roles and responsibilities.

"Tell me about yourself," is a gateway to intentionally position your value to an employer. In the absence of thoughtfully answering this question, you leave the answer to "Who are you?" solely up to the employer based on questions of their choosing.

You should be able to clearly, confidently, and succinctly explain your value in thirty seconds or less. If you are not able to do this, you're not ready for prime time.

> *TIP #1:* Know yourself. Your strengths, personality, and competency assessments are a great way to learn more about what makes you unique. This understanding equips you to incorporate your assets into your cover letter, resume, networking conversations, and respond to the inquiry, "Tell me about yourself."

> *TIP #2:* You must be able to illustrate to an employer that what you do best is what they need. If what you have to offer doesn't add value to an employer, they won' be buying what you're selling, and that's YOU.

■ ■ ■

Because only 25 percent of people know their strengths, fewer still have translated top strengths into a value statement.

■ ■ ■

The truth is, many interviewers ask this question, and you should be prepared to answer it without merely reciting your job history. That's boring. Even worse, saying *"I've been a project manager for ten years"* doesn't tell anything about why you're a *good* project manager. *What value do you bring?*

Defining value statements
Your value statement, sometimes referred to as a value proposition, is simply the primary benefit you can bring an employer.

Why have a value statement?

Value statements:

- Can answer the question, "Why should I hire you?"
- Provide an opportunity to explain what makes you unique.
- Frame your strengths in networking or exploratory conversations.
- Provide great language for your LinkedIn profile summary.
- Can be leveraged in your resume and cover letter.
- Demonstrate that you are clear about who you are.
- Set you apart because most people don't have one.
- Display confidence.
- Need more reasons? I could continue, but let's get down to brass tacks.

Example value statements

Here are some example value statements of people who know the strengths they want to highlight to employers.

"I have confidence, drive and courage to take risks, overcome problems, and take on new ideas. My communication skills, flexibility, adaptability, enthusiasm, and optimism translate to social ease within and across teams."

"I'm an innovator. I have a natural tendency to come up with new ideas and combinations of ideas spontaneously to solve complex problems. I'm able to identify solutions that lead to success and turn those solutions into actionable steps that bring about excellence. My strong communication skills ensure I effectively manage change throughout a transformation."

"I analyze and strategize before taking action. In my work, I'm organized and structured and can be counted on. I set high standards for myself and believe I can achieve them. I scan available ideas and concepts, weighing them against a current strategy, and plan for every conceivable contingency."

You should have two versions of your value statement, one spoken and one written. If you write your value statement and try to share it orally, it might come across unnatural, formal, and awkward.

Here's an example:

> *Interviewer:* Tell me about yourself.
>
> *Interviewee:* I build strong cross-functional relationships through empathy, rapport-building, and communication skills. I excel at achieving consensus by fostering collaboration. These strengths have helped me gain buy-in and influence people who don't actually report to me. Because most project problems are people problems, I have a high project success rate as a project manager because of these strengths.

Personally, I'd like to hire a person who desires to bring value to me as an employer. It's certainly more compelling than, "I have ten years of experience as a project manager."

The best advice I can give is that your value statement must be comfortable for you. You are going to speak it, so it should feel natural.

Creating your value statement

1. Make a list of words that are true of you.

Using feedback you've repeatedly heard from others, assessments you've taken, and self-evaluation, generate a list of words or short phrases to describe yourself. Would you include responsible, achievement-oriented, peace-maker, negotiator, idea-generator, problem-solver, accurate, diversity-oriented, safety-conscious, self-confident, learning agile, comfortable with ambiguity, motivates others, entrepreneurial, diplomatic, or organized? What else would you include?

2. Cross out ambiguous or cliché words, such as "team player", and choose words that are specific. What makes you a team player? Are

you collaborative? Do you listen well? Are you empathetic? Do you have strong accountability? Say that, instead.

3. Ask others the following:
   - What are three words that describe me?
   - What am I good at?

When writing this book, I asked my husband two questions. He responded:

Three words to describe me: *passionate, dedicated, visionary*
What am I good at? *reading and understanding people*

I created a sample value statement using his feedback.

> *Using my ability to read and understand people, I help my clients increase their self-awareness, see their value, and cast a vision for their future. My passion and dedication inspire them to strive to reach their visions and fulfill their potential.*

I wrote that in four seconds, but I hope it demonstrates potential to help you express the value you bring. Drafting a value statement is a great starting point to craft and hone your message. You can also think of a story that backs up what you're saying by briefly telling the interviewer about a time you demonstrated the strengths you shared with them.

I would not have thought of those words, nor would I have answered what I'm good at the same way without asking for feedback. The perspective of others is invaluable. Tap into it.

4. After you've drafted your message, practice aloud. If it doesn't flow, rewrite the message until it feels natural.
5. Tell someone else. Practice your value statement on your partner or a close friend. Ask for feedback, adjust, and repeat.

Now, I leave you with the question. What's your value? Take some time to write your value statement now.

Tell me about a time you made a mistake

Do you admit and take responsibility for your mistakes or blame others? Do you repeat your mistakes or learn from them? That's primarily what your future employer wants to know. To best answer this question, think of a time you made a mistake that wasn't enormous or disastrous.

Make sure you convey that you took ownership and share any lessons learned or steps you took to ensure you didn't repeat the mistake. Did you put something in place to prevent the mistake in the future?

Ultimately, your answer to this question should convey three things: accountability, a lesson learned, and steps taken to prevent it happening again.

Tell me about a conflict you've had with a boss or a co-worker

If you state you've never had a conflict with a co-worker, an employer might be suspicious and think you're avoiding the subject or not being honest.

If you truly have not had a conflict with a co-worker (though conflict can be as simple as a difference of opinion about how to approach a project or problem), be prepared to explain your characteristics or strategies that contribute to peaceful working relationships.

For example, are you high in empathy and able to identify if you're upsetting someone, then quickly recover the conversation? Are you flexible, open-minded, and hard to offend?

If you can recall a conflict in the workplace, do not go into a lot of detail or gossip-like characterization of the circumstances. Briefly describe the conflict and what steps you took to resolve it.

A willingness to apologize, admit mistakes, and address conflict in a mature and positive way is desirable to employers.

Can you tell me about this gap in your employment on your resume?

I've worked with people many times who have gaps on their resumes, from role mismatches or interpersonal conflict that resulted in their termination to health situations, and even time spent in prison. Gaps are not the end of the world, but you must handle them wisely.

If you have had a termination due to personality conflicts, performance issues, or other role or cultural fit reasons, it's best to be forthright and honest, "My previous job/employer was not a fit, but I learned a lot from the experience, such as doing my homework to find the right fit. And that is why I'm excited about this opportunity."

Never say anything negative about your previous manager or employers.

If your employment gap is related to a conviction resulting in prison time, your best bet is to be honest with the employer that you had a lapse in judgment and focus on what you've learned from the experience. However, limit the details of your offense and focus on the lessons learned and how you've changed as a person.

The people I've met who have made mistakes are more determined not to repeat them. If that describes you, let the manager know you will work harder than most because you recognize you must earn people's trust due to your mistake.

If you have a gap of employment due to health problems, it is sufficient to say a family priority necessitated a sabbatical from your employment.

Regardless of the sticky question you might be asked, honesty is the best policy. But avoid sharing specific details. Stay at a high level and focus on positive outcomes.

After you've aced your interview, it's time to seal the deal with your follow up.

STEP 4

I HAD MY INTERVIEW. NOW WHAT? SURPRISE THEM!

The best approach you can take post-interview is a proactive one. Many candidates take a passive sit-and-wait-to-hear-back approach. Being proactive takes away that helpless feeling of waiting and positions you in a positive light to the employer. Surprise them by being different from the pack.

Before reviewing post-interview best-practices, I must emphasize that you should keep job searching, keep interviewing, and keep moving prospects forward until you have an offer *in writing*. Job seeker Cheryl shared the following with me:

> In my most recent experience, I waited more than a month for the second interview to be organized, and when I finally met the local manager during the interview he said, "You got the job," but after more than a week waiting the HR guy told me they decided to go for someone more experienced.

In my line of work, I hear numerous stories of retracted oral offers. A former client shared the time her daughter was given an oral offer, along with a link to do an online assessment. She gave two weeks' notice at her current job, then the new employer rescinded the offer based on test results. She was not informed that the offer was contingent upon the test.

When she approached her employer to retract her notice, she learned they had already given her position to someone else.

Bottom line: Do <u>not</u> give notice to your current employer or halt your job search until a written offer has been extended and accepted.

Until you get that offer letter, here are five things you can do after you've had the hiring manager interview. This might be your second interview if you've already had a human resources phone screen.

Follow up

The same day of your interview, send a thank you email to the hiring manager and consider mailing a thank you note. You can ask the recruiter for contact information or to pass on your handwritten note to the recruiter if they won't release the contact information.

A handwritten note is optional in select cases. I had a client once tell me written cards would not be viewed positively in a research institution setting, so I told him he should go with his instinct.

When composing your note, if you're interested in the position, say so. If not, simply thank them for their time. Sending a note expressing disinterest in the role is unnecessary unless you're faced with an offer. If another position you're interested in becomes available, you want to retain positive connections in the company.

The brief email should contain one connection between what you bring to the position and something they mentioned they're looking for in the selected candidate. Include the connection only if you're interested in the role.

Sample email if you're <u>not</u> interested:

> Dear Ms. Jones,
> Thank you for meeting with me to discuss the Human Resources Business Partner position. I was pleased to meet you, and I truly appreciate your time today.
> Best regards,
> Jane Doe

Sample email if you <u>are</u> interested:

> Dear Ms. Jones,
>
> Thank you for your time today to discuss the Human Resources Business Partner position. I was pleased to meet you and to learn about what you're seeking to accomplish through this role. After hearing your description of the successful candidate, I'm confident my ability to build strong relationships across an organization and my political savvy to navigate all levels of a company signal me as a solid candidate. I will follow up with you next week to inquire about the status of my candidacy.
>
> Best regards,
>
> Jane Doe

Follow up once weekly by email to inquire on the status of the position. During your follow-up you might share an interesting article based on something you discussed with the hiring manager or an article in the news about the employer with a positive comment. I recommend following up for four weeks.

> Dear Ms. Jones,
>
> I hope you are doing well and having a great week. I am following up to express my continued interest in the Human Resources Business Partner role and to discover the status of my candidacy for the position.
>
> Based on our discussion of the importance of customer service, I thought you'd enjoy this article. <Insert URL>
>
> I look forward to hearing from you.
>
> Best regards,
>
> Jane Doe

The exception to the weekly follow up rule is if you're given a follow up schedule by the hiring manager. For example, if they say please contact me again in two weeks, wait two weeks as directed.

Prepare for the salary discussion

Ideally you should research salary prior to applying and interviewing for a position, but if you haven't completed that step don't worry. However, you don't want to be caught unprepared with an offer on the table and no time to research salary information.

Some salary research tools are:

- www.salary.com
- www.onetonline.org
- www.glassdoor.com

Below are two resources to help you prepare for the salary conversation.

- The Exact Words to Use When Negotiating Salary
  tinyurl.com/y98md3xg
- Five Steps to Help Calculate Your Asking Salary
  www.salary.com/5-ways-what-youre-worth/

Prepare for the next step in the process

If you work in a field where testing is likely, you might consider working on sample projects to be more prepared. For example, if you're a technical person and it's been a while since you've interviewed, you could conduct an online search for sample interview tests for your field.

If you're in marketing, sales, or training, you might be asked to give a presentation. Ensure your presentation skills are up to snuff.

If you work in communications, instructional design, or a field with writing or design samples, ensure you've selected something stellar from your portfolio if you are invited to the next round of interviews. You might have provided a work sample earlier in the process, but show you have the skill and ambition to bring another.

Some employers provide a scenario and ask candidates to create a proposal, strategy, or solution to aid their final hiring selection. Do your best to research the interview tactics common for the organization interviewing you by using the research websites above or search common interview formats for your field. This is especially important if you have not interviewed in a while because processes change with time.

If you've taken personality tests in the past that would illustrate a good fit for the role, offer to share the results.

Contact your references

Consider having at least three professional references. Call or email your potential references and ask if they are willing to provide a positive recommendation for you. Think about the aspects of the job where they will be knowledgeable about your performance and character and give them an overview of the position so they can connect what they know about you to the job when the potential employer contacts them.

Finally, only if an offer is extended, you might want to ask the new employer if you could speak to a couple of team members if you have remaining questions before deciding on the offer.

Make an offer

This approach is not right for everyone and is best suited for certain kinds of positions or roles that can be performed as a consultant or contractor.

After meeting with the hiring manager, you could create a proposal that addresses a need they have, how you plan to resolve their need, a time estimate to implement the solution, what results they will receive, and the cost or fees they should expect to pay.

For example, if you notice they could use some help with their LinkedIn or Facebook company page and you possess these skills, you could submit a proposal to perform value-added services to improve their internet or social media presence.

Alternatively, if during the interview the hiring manager shared something he or she is trying to accomplish through the role, you could submit a one-page proposal outlining how you'd tackle the problem and request an opportunity to discuss it. You don't need to have all the details. They'll be impressed with your initiative.

Be proactive after the interview to ensure you're better prepared for the next step, demonstrate an action-oriented approach, and set yourself apart from the candidates who are quietly waiting in the wings!

Next, we'll discuss what to do if you are getting interviews but no offers.

STEP 5

NO OFFERS? TEN SURPRISING REASONS WHY

If you've had several interviews and you're not getting offers, especially if you're not moving past the first round, an important step in the job search process is reflecting on your interviews to evaluate what you are doing well, not so well, and what you need to do differently next time.

Engage in mock interviews with someone who will give you straight and honest feedback.

The number one reason candidates are passed up for a role is failure to differentiate themselves from other candidates. Therefore, being memorable (for the right reasons) is a winning strategy.

However, sometimes factors are at play that we're not consciously aware of. Unfortunately, most employers won't openly provide feedback about your habits, quirks, or perceived warts.

A few years ago, I had a prospective client contact me because he wasn't getting job offers. He had impressive experience and was getting invited to a lot of interviews, yet every opportunity died on the interview table in the first round. He assumed he was doing something wrong, but what?

As a coach, I've learned to tell hard truths, with compassion, to people because it's in their best interest.

Following are issues I've encountered both as an interviewer and obstacles I've helped clients overcome. The list is not exhaustive, but it represents the most common problems I've seen.

Carrying anger or negativity forward from a previous position

Were you laid off after twenty years of loyal service, fired by a manager who wanted to give the job to their friend, forced to train your off-shore replacement, or some other disappointing circumstance?

It's essential you let it go. Today.

Communication is only 7 percent words. Any root of bitterness in you is detectable in your tone and body language by an interviewer, even if you're unaware of what you're projecting. The only way to truly let a grudge against a former employer go is to forgive the person who wronged you and move on.

You're not forgiving them for their benefit. You're doing it for yourself. Living with resentment or anger toward someone gives them power over you. Don't give them that control.

Off-putting personality traits

The person I was telling you about who wasn't getting offers? He suspected he was doing something to put people off.

My client's initial attitude was, "I'm going to be myself and if people don't like me, too bad. I don't want to work there if I have to fake who I am to get hired."

If being a likable human being requires faking, you must address the problem.

A woman at a networking event I attended mirrored his sentiment. She said, "People don't need to like me. We just need to be able to work together." While not everyone is going to like you, proclaiming you don't care if people like you implies you commonly encounter dislike.

Hiring managers have plenty of candidates to choose from whom they can work well with... and like.

If you share this attitude, remember that everything happens through people. Expecting others to accommodate a bad attitude when you're not accommodating what they need from you is an unrealistic expectation.

In the long run, it's more work dealing with the conflict a bad attitude creates in your life than the effort to transform your attitude. You don't want to be the reason you don't succeed.

Some other off-putting personality traits in an interview are arrogance, humble bragging, defensiveness, excessive nervousness, and lack of confidence.

I'm happy to report I did some interview coaching with my client and the next interview resulted in an offer. I did, however, provide some tough love on what would be necessary to ensure he retained his employment.

Appearing unprepared

My sister-in-law, Grace, shared the following story with me.

> I once interviewed a recent college graduate for a medical photography position. He had photography experience but had never done medical photography. He did well on the first interview. We narrowed our group and invited him back.
>
> On his second interview, we asked if he had researched the position more and what it would entail, if he had looked up medical photographs to get an idea of what kind of images he would be taking, etc. His response? "I looked up how much money they make, that's it."
>
> We were not impressed.

Follow the suggestions in Step II to demonstrate to interviewers that preparedness is a priority to you.

Brutal honesty

Always be truthful in an interview. However, evaluate if what you are about to share is too much information. I interviewed a woman and asked her to share one area in which she felt she needed personal or professional development. She told me she had a bad temper. I wasn't keen to experience it. Be honest, but don't be brutally honest. That's simply sabotage.

Manner of speech: Mumbling, talking too fast or too slow

Many interviews start with a phone screen. Once, I provided telephone coaching to a client whom I struggled to understand because he mumbled. One day I asked him, "Has anyone ever given you feedback that it's difficult to understand you over the phone? You mumble and speak rapidly, and I can see this being an obstacle for you—especially in a phone interview."

No one had spoken truth to this man about his mumbling. Simple awareness of his issue enabled him to speak more clearly and slow down. After more than a year of unemployment, he landed a job in less than a month.

University of Michigan researchers have found people who talk fast are seen as out to pull the wool over our eyes, while people who talk slowly are seen as not too bright or tiresome.

Remember to slow your speech slightly if you have an accent the interviewer might not be familiar with. Practice answering interview questions with people who are willing to tell you the truth if you're speaking too fast or too slowly. Creating a video with a smart phone is the best way to view your interview performance.

What it something I said?

Share your interview answers with a few reasonable and level-headed people for their reactions. If you're not getting offers, you might be saying something that is preventing you from moving to the next round.

Nicole, a former colleague, shared this story with me:

> I was interviewing a man who was telling about a time when he had to alert his senior leadership of risks to a project's success. As he explained, he meant to say, "The risks were real and imminent." Instead, he said "The risks were real and impotent." He used the word "impotent" several times instead of imminent. Know your big words when using them!

Hiring manager, Tyna, had this to share:

> An interviewee came to the interview thinking they were interviewing for another position. When I broke the news, the response was, "That's okay. I'm looking for something to pay the bills."
>
> Another interviewee showed up ten minutes late, unapologetic, and during the interview her cell phone kept going off. She then answered a question and proceeded to ask me, "Was that a good answer?"
>
> Next, please!

Jacquie shared this story:

> I was hiring an engineer. This man came to the office dressed appropriately, highly educated, on time, and I was excited to talk to him. I won't drone on about the details but he made three negative remarks about women. The first was about our lack of ability to drive in the snow. The second was about him expecting his dinner in the microwave waiting for him, lastly was that I must have a hard time in the industry, being a woman and all. I told him I had all the information I needed and ended the interview. He asked about next steps. I told him this was the end of the line. He was surprised.

Finally, hiring manager, Emily, had this to say:

> I had one [interviewee] where their current employer was my former employer. I asked him a question about his current job and his response was, "I know who you are."
>
> Creepy. I did not hire him.

Chronically Late?

Some interviewers might be gracious if you're late for an interview, but the consensus is most find tardiness unacceptable. Always allow enough time to arrive a few minutes early for an interview despite traffic delays. Getting lost is never a good excuse, as you should take a dry run to the location ahead of your interview. Large companies can have sprawling campuses and trying to find your way at the time of the interview will cause nothing but stress.

I once read a post on LinkedIn from a gentleman who was late to an interview because a motorcyclist was killed on the highway right in front of him, which he shared upon arriving late. After he was passed up for the role, the feedback was that he was late for the interview.

My sister-in-law, Grahame, once had an interviewee show up late with no explanation or apology and then argued that he was still entitled to an interview. You can imagine how well that went over.

If you often run late, leave a half hour earlier than you normally would. It's better to sit and wait than to walk in late.

Rambling

I once interviewed someone who spent twenty-five minutes of a thirty-minute phone screen answering only the first question I asked. I writhed in pain in my chair, and the only thought going through my head was that weekly one-on-ones with him would be torture.

Rambling can be caused by nervousness, lack of preparation, a misguided opinion that the interviewer requires every detail of your story, or unfamiliarity with best practices for answering interview questions.

One way to avoid rambling is to use the S.T.A.R. technique to ensure succinct and targeted answers to questions. "Step II: Storytelling with S.T.A.R" explains this method. You should also prepare a list of your top performance results linked to what the employer seeks in the job description. Detailed instructions are found in "Step II: The Role Mapping Technique."

Lack of Passion

I've had more than one client tell me the feedback they received from an employer was that they weren't selected because they didn't seem interested in the position. One of my clients really wanted the job, so she was surprised at this feedback.

Unfortunately, we do seem to have an extroversion bias in the hiring process, with some exceptions in introversion-dominated fields such as IT and engineering, because extroverts more easily connect with interviewers and demonstrate passion and engagement. However, you can demonstrate authentic interest with words instead of elevated energy levels.

For instance, smiling and stating you're interested in the position after what you've heard is a perfect way to demonstrate passion for a role. When you never smile or express any passion whatsoever, the interviewer might interpret boredom and disinterest, even if that's not what you meant to convey.

Make clear to the interviewer that you want the job in a way that is comfortable and authentic to you.

Failure to stand out from the other candidates

When we read a position description, our perfect fit is obvious to us. However, a hiring manager lacks the context you have about your own experiences and skills. The only information they have is the resume you provided, which you hope connected your specific experiences and results to their needs. Remember, the resume gets you the interview, but the interview gets you the job.

Failure to stand out by demonstrating a clear picture of what you offer, by connecting what you do best to what the employer needs most, can cost you. Refer to "Step II: The Role Mapping Technique" for specific guidance.

Excessive nervousness or lack of confidence

Have you visited a friend or family member with a dog that gets so nervous when people enter the house it starts to shake and urinate on the floor? It's pitiful, isn't it?

As a hiring manager, I interviewed a lot of people, and many were nervous. While being nervous in an interview is normal, the image of the shaking, squirting little dog should not come to a hiring manager's mind when interviewing you!

Nerves detectable by an interviewer are self-sabotaging. The thought of sabotaging yourself should make you more nervous than participating in the interview.

The human brain is a three-pound organ of survival. Most people are wired to seek comfort and familiarity. The fear center of the brain, the amygdala, kicks into gear any time we're in situations that are unfamiliar or uncomfortable. Interviews are one of the least comfortable things we do in our careers.

I've read a lot of advice on calming interview nerves yet have not found a lot of discussion on *why* we're nervous in the first place. Understanding why you're nervous can help you overcome it. I've determined three main drivers behind interview nerves, though not all three might apply to you.

Reason #1: Status

Our tendency is to place ourselves and others in a social hierarchy. In an interview setting, we are not the alpha. We view ourselves in this setting as lower in the hierarchy. When we mentally subordinate ourselves to interviewers, we place ourselves at a lower value.

What can you do about it? View the interviewer as your peer, in other words, your equal. They do have equal value to you as a person. So, try to think of them as a person, rather than their title.

According to David Rock, head of the NeuroLeadership Institute, the strongest threats and rewards are social. Social threats and rewards significantly activate the brain's pain/pleasure center. Therefore, this status trigger results in a threat response. We're uncomfortable because our perceived lower status is highlighted in an interview situation.

Reason #2: Uncertainty

Interviews lack transparency. We don't have insight into what the interviewer thinks about us, and we're performing for them but receiving minimal real-time feedback. We also don't know what we're going to be asked.

Will I be caught off guard with a question? Will I be asked something I always struggle to answer, such as the reason for leaving my last job? Will another opportunity present itself anytime soon if I blow this one?

The best way to overcome uncertainty is to be as prepared as possible. If you struggle to answer specific questions, you must practice answering them and ask a few people you respect to provide their input.

The next best way to be more comfortable with uncertainty is to learn to be comfortable in your own skin. If you can build your own confidence, you'll be less concerned about what an interviewer thinks of you. How do you build your confidence? A great start is completing the "List Your Assets: Inventorying Your Strengths" exercise in Step II.

In my experience, when my clients take time to understand how they are unique and the contributions they can bring, their confidence increases. You might not believe it right now, but you are a masterpiece. No one has the same life experiences, interests, skills, personality, gifting, and strengths you do. No one. Countless clients have told me one of the biggest outcomes of working together to discover their talents is the gain in their confidence.

Reason #3: Control

Finally, a job interview creates a control threat, because the interviewer controls both the interview and the hiring outcome. In the interview setting, we perceive we're not holding any power. To hold power, we must reject feelings of overwhelm and take control of the situation. Be decisive and add value. Powerlessness is just another form of fear.

Many researchers have used exposure therapy to reduce fear in subjects.

In an interview with *Outside Online*, neuroscientist Sian Beilock explained what happens when people take math tests:

> *Most people experience math anxiety. Their cortisol levels rise, and their misery and self-doubt inhibit their working memory, causing them to perform worse than they would otherwise. But an interesting thing happens to people who are confident in their math skills: The cortisol makes them do better. They become more focused.*

These findings are just as applicable to interview skills as to math skills.

Self-awareness, preparation, and practice are the keys to unlock confidence and comfort in interview settings.

Having a coachable spirit and being open to feedback is vital. After several interviews with no offer, I recommend participating in mock interviews and seeking feedback to discover if you're making any of the above blunders. Perhaps other candidates were simply more qualified, but it can't hurt to shine a light into all the corners to be certain you're not tripping yourself with these common mistakes.

Because nervousness is a common concern, and one of the most difficult to overcome, spending some additional time addressing why interview nerves are harmful and strategies you can employ to better control them is time well invested.

Three ways nerves affect your interview

Interviewer Confidence

Visible nerves undermine the interviewer's confidence in you and call your competence into question. If you aren't confident in your ability to do the job, the hiring manager has no reason to be.

Visible nerves give the impression you can't handle pressure situations. Your manager won't be comfortable giving you challenges, putting you in front of clients, asking you to give presentations, or anything that could potentially undermine confidence in his or her team.

Failed Rapport-Building

Nerves distract both you and the interviewer from building rapport. An interviewee has two goals during an interview: connect your abilities to the position and connect with the interviewer.

Nerves don't materialize out of thin air. They result from anxiety-provoking thoughts in your mind. Get out of your head and focus on the interviewer, because self-focus blocks rapport.

Degraded Performance

When we feel fearful, our brains have alerted us to danger. Short of spotting a venomous snake in your chair, an interview is not a dangerous situation, and turning it into one puts your body into fight/flight mode.

What happens when you're in fight/flight?

The stress hormone, cortisol, is released into your bloodstream causing your hands to become cold and sweaty (not pleasant to shake), your mouth to become dry (not easy to speak eloquently with a dry mouth), and the pre-frontal cortex to experience lower levels of oxygen. Lower oxygen impairs your ability to recall stories in behavior interviews with questions such as, "Tell me about a time when..."

Decreased oxygen in your pre-frontal cortex also impairs social interactions, your ability to portray your authentic personality, and clear thinking. Therefore, some people say irrational things when upset or stressed.

Strategies to keep your nerves in check

Take slow, deep breaths

Oxygenate your brain so you can think clearly.

Before going into your interview take three slow, deep breaths, holding them for a count of three, then slowly release. This helps oxygenate your brain. Yawning also accomplishes oxygenation.

Reframe fear as positive energy

Pay attention to the thoughts going through your mind.

Most likely your subconscious thoughts will carry your confidence away like a runaway train. Consciously identifying your thoughts allows you to challenge those thoughts and counter-balance them with different thinking, not accepting them at face value.

Example:

> "So much is riding on this job. If I don't get it, I can't pay my rent."

I'm willing to bet you're not homeless, and if it came right down to it you have friends or family who aren't going to stand by and watch you live in an alley if you don't get that job. When the thought surfaces, you must reassure yourself the right job for you is out there. And when the right job presents, you're going to get it.

I work with clients who are beyond miserable and gainfully employed. Not receiving an offer means you weren't what they were looking for. But you're exactly what someone else needs. Count your blessings you avoided a situation as bad, or worse, than the situation you're in.

Think positive thoughts

The brain can't focus on a negative and a positive at the same time. Knowing this, focus on your positives, those strengths that make you stand out. Everyone has strengths and, in fact, only one in thirty-three million people share the same top five in common on the Clifton StrengthsFinder assessment.

I highly recommend taking the assessment at www.gallupstrengths-center.com and learning how to apply your strengths to speak more confidently about your strengths. "Section II: I have my top five strengths. Now what?" details how to do this.

Another positive approach is to tell the interviewer how glad you are to meet them, and that you're looking forward to this time together. You'd be surprised how you can convince your brain that you really are happy to be in the situation.

Laugh a little and smile

Just as adrenaline has a negative effect on interview performance, positive neurochemicals, which are released when you laugh and smile, have a positive effect. People who smile and laugh are rated higher in likability, and a lot of research suggests that smiles are contagious. When I was in Walmart in Nashville, Tennessee, the cashier didn't look at me or address me when I was checking out. At the end of the transaction she looked up at me to give me the receipt. When she looked at me, I gave her a genuine, big smile.

Her hard exterior immediately melted and she returned a big smile back at me. It was a thing of beauty.

Expose your fear
Creating transparency in an interview setting helps you face a fear head on. The second benefit is that when you admit vulnerability, you create trust through authenticity. Ask the interviewer for feedback on your nerves. Here is an example of how to broach the subject:

> *Interviewer:* How are you today?
> *You:* I'm well, though, I'm admittedly nervous in interviews and I'm challenging myself to improve. Would you be open to giving me feedback at the end of the interview on displaying nervousness? I know this might seem difficult, but it will be worth it.

Do your homework
We rise (or fall) to our level of preparedness.

Make sure you are prepared to interview for the position, as preparation is a key defense to nerves. You will want to be intentional in preparing for each specific job interview.

Exercise, get plenty of rest the night before, eat breakfast
Our coping skills suffer when we're not well-rested or nourished. Exercising the day before your interview should help you sleep better that night so you feel ready to go.

Think before you speak
If you're nervous, you're at risk of rambling. Poor impressions are certain to be made if the interviewer is subjected to a flood of poorly thought out responses. If you don't have an answer ready, ask for a moment to give the question some thought or ask to return to the question at the end. Five to ten seconds should give you enough time to consider your answer.

ASSESSING AN OFFER

After you receive that coveted offer, you should consider a few things. Ideally, you should prepare a list of your must-haves and deal breakers prior to receiving an offer to help you make an objective decision.

Career fulfillment seems to evade many people. In fact, Gallup reports 52 percent of people would quit their jobs tomorrow if they could. After speaking to hundreds of clients, I've found the key conditions for career and job satisfaction tend to be:

- Aligning your *values* to your work, your manager, and the company you work for
- Calling upon your *strengths* daily in your work
- Using the *skills* you enjoy, while avoiding or limiting the skills that burn you out
- Doing work that aligns to your *passion* or *interests*

Therefore, in addition to evaluating the compensation package and benefits, commute, and other factors, make sure to evaluate the opportunity against your values, strengths, skills, and interests.

You can use the information you create in the *List Your Assets* exercise from Step II as a blueprint to evaluate offers, along with the values exercise available for download at:

tinyurl.com/y8zy5z2j

FINAL THOUGHTS

Few people look forward to, or enjoy, job interviews. In fact, the entire job search process can be one of the most frustrating, demotivating, and discouraging experiences of your adult life. If you employ the advice and tools contained in this book, along with the free "Interview Prep Kit," you are likely to significantly shorten the duration of your job search process to land the job you want, faster.

If you would like interview preparation assistance, please contact me at *ksherry@virtuscareers.com*, and remember to download your free Interview Prep Kit at resources.virtuscareers.com/interview-prep-kit.

I wish you all the best in your next interview!

TOOLS AND GOODIES

Interview Prep Kit
Download your free "Interview Prep Kit" at resources.virtuscareers.com/interview-prep-kit

LinkedIn Profile Optimization for Dummies by Donna Serdula
tinyurl.com/yczqx96w

How to Create an All-Star LinkedIn Profile
tinyurl.com/ycp7rndk

Free LinkedIn Headline Generator Tool
tinyurl.com/y86veslr

Skill-based Cover Letter Template
tinyurl.com/y7medlyp

Employer-focused Cover Letters
tinyurl.com/ydbzzwud

ACKNOWLEDGEMENTS

To God for His goodness and love in my life.

To my amazing clients who entrusted me with their careers. I do not take this honor lightly.

To my editor and friend Beth Crosby who is a pleasure to work with. Her dedication, commitment to excellence, and accountability is unparalleled.

To my colleague Brian Ray for generously writing the foreword of this book and who has always been willing to lend an ear, eye, or hand to my projects.

ABOUT THE AUTHOR

Kristin Sherry is a Career and Executive Coach, Founder of Virtus Career Consulting, speaker, and author of the career empowerment book, *Follow Your Star: Career Lessons I Learned from Mom.*

 Formerly, Kristin served as a Learning & Development leader at a Fortune 20 company where she managed the company's learning strategy and coached leaders and their teams to increased effectiveness.

Kristin works with both companies and individuals in the areas of career management, career discovery and transition; and leadership and team development. She is currently the leadership coach for AmerisourceBergen's (NYSE: ABC) emerging leader and senior leader development programs.

Kristin holds ten coaching, leadership development, and behavioral assessment certifications. She has written numerous career-related articles published in a dozen countries and read by more than a million people and speaks at conferences and workshops across the United States. She also continues to serve in the Crossroads Career Ministry as a volunteer career coach.

Kristin lives in Wesley Chapel, North Carolina, with her husband Xander and their four children.

Follow Kristin and Virtus Career Consulting on Social Media!
Twitter: @virtus_careers
Instagram: @virtuscareers
Facebook: www.facebook.com/virtuscareers
LinkedIn: www.linkedin.com/in/kristinsherry

Book Kristin for Speaking Engagements or Workshops
www.virtuscareers.com/contact-us
Conferences and Keynotes
Networking Events
Workshops
Podcasts

Made in the USA
Monee, IL
28 February 2020